Huge Hamburger

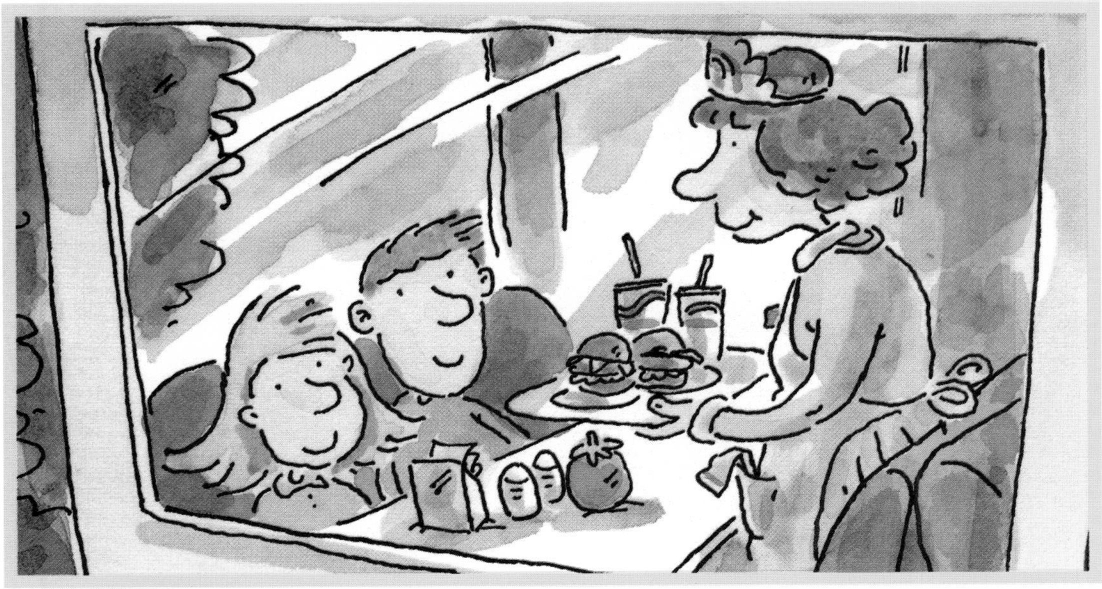

Written by Rosann Englebretson
Illustrated by Colin Paine

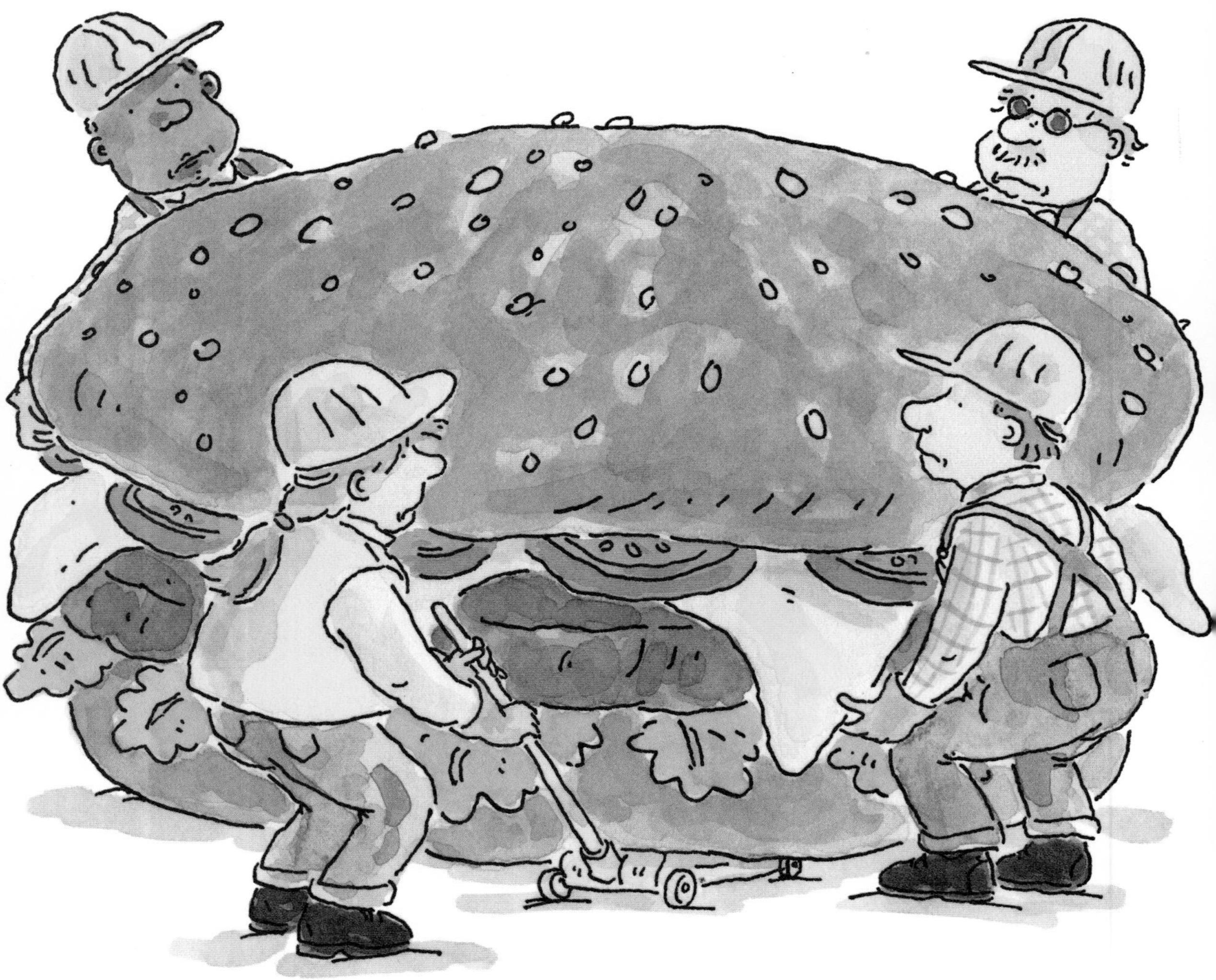

Huge hamburger.

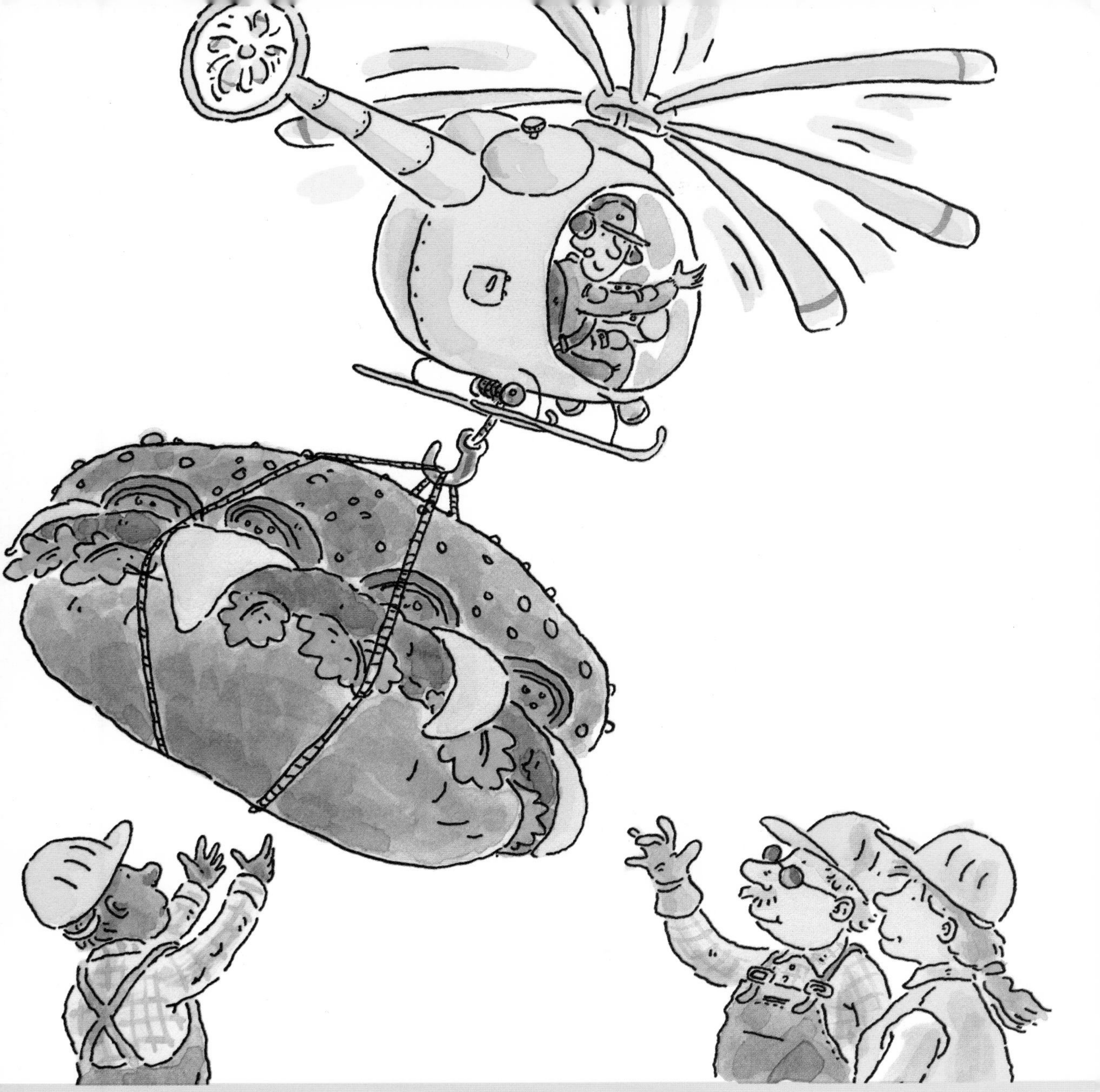

Huge hamburger.

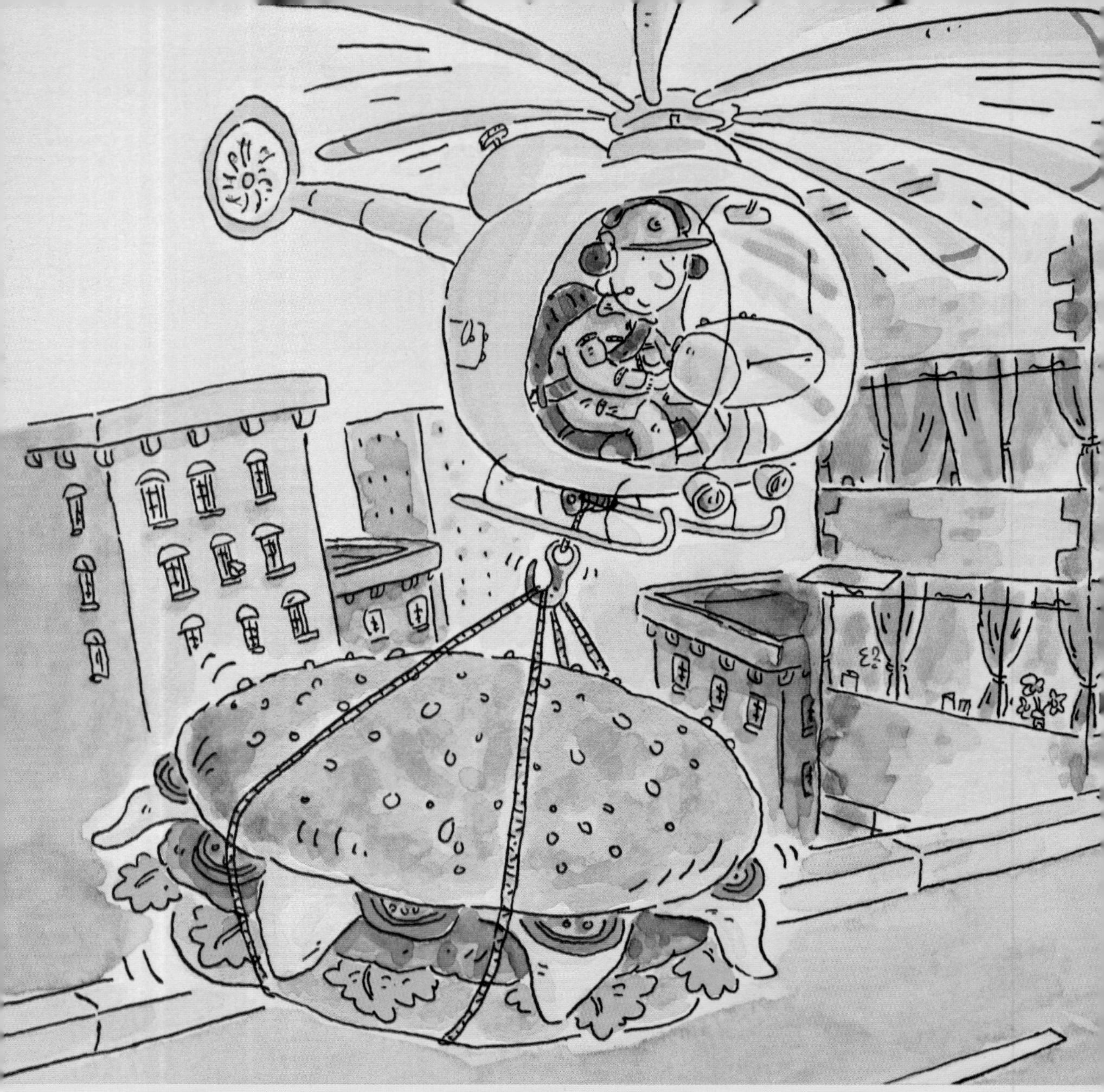

Huge hamburger.

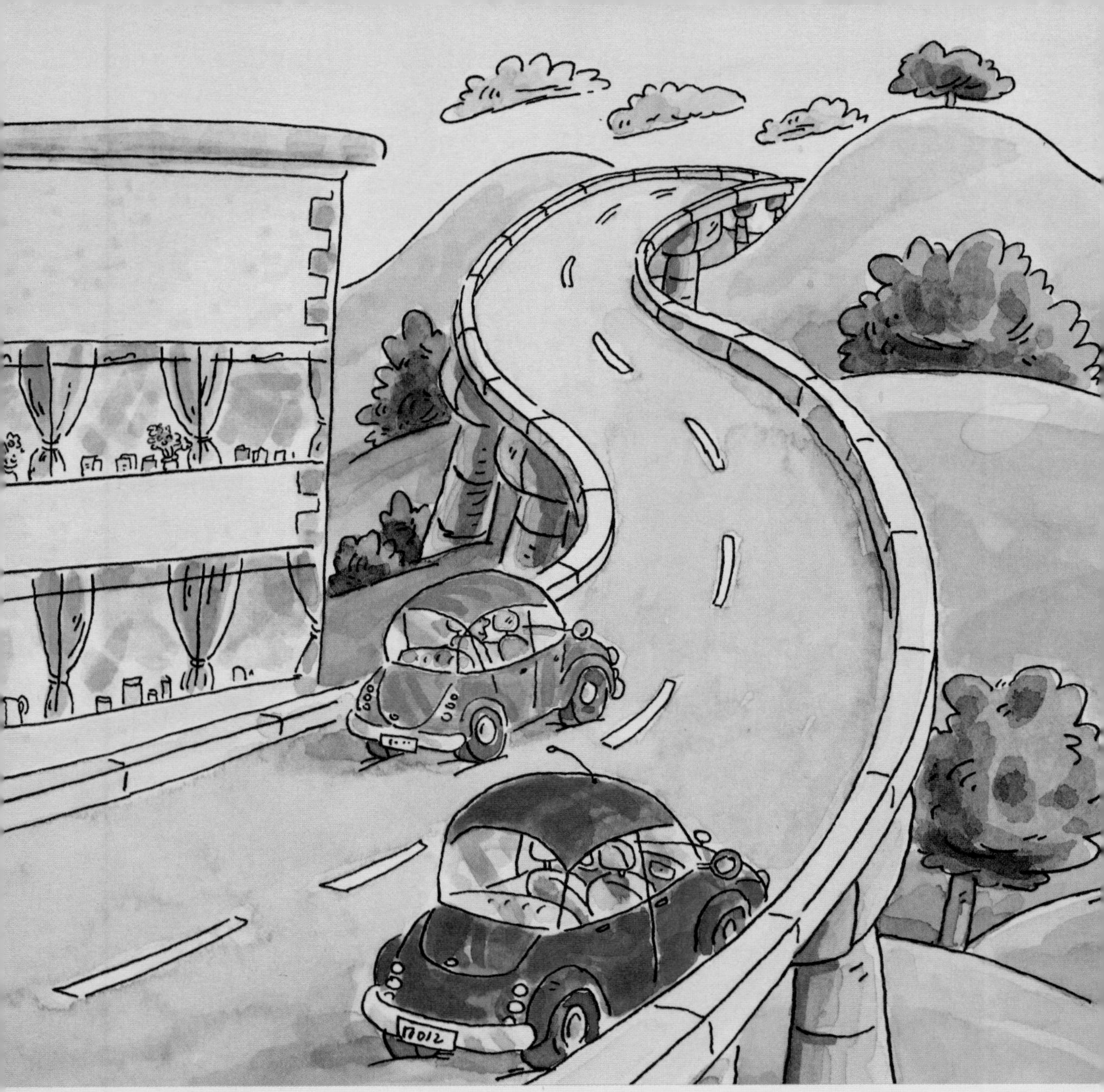
Π0012

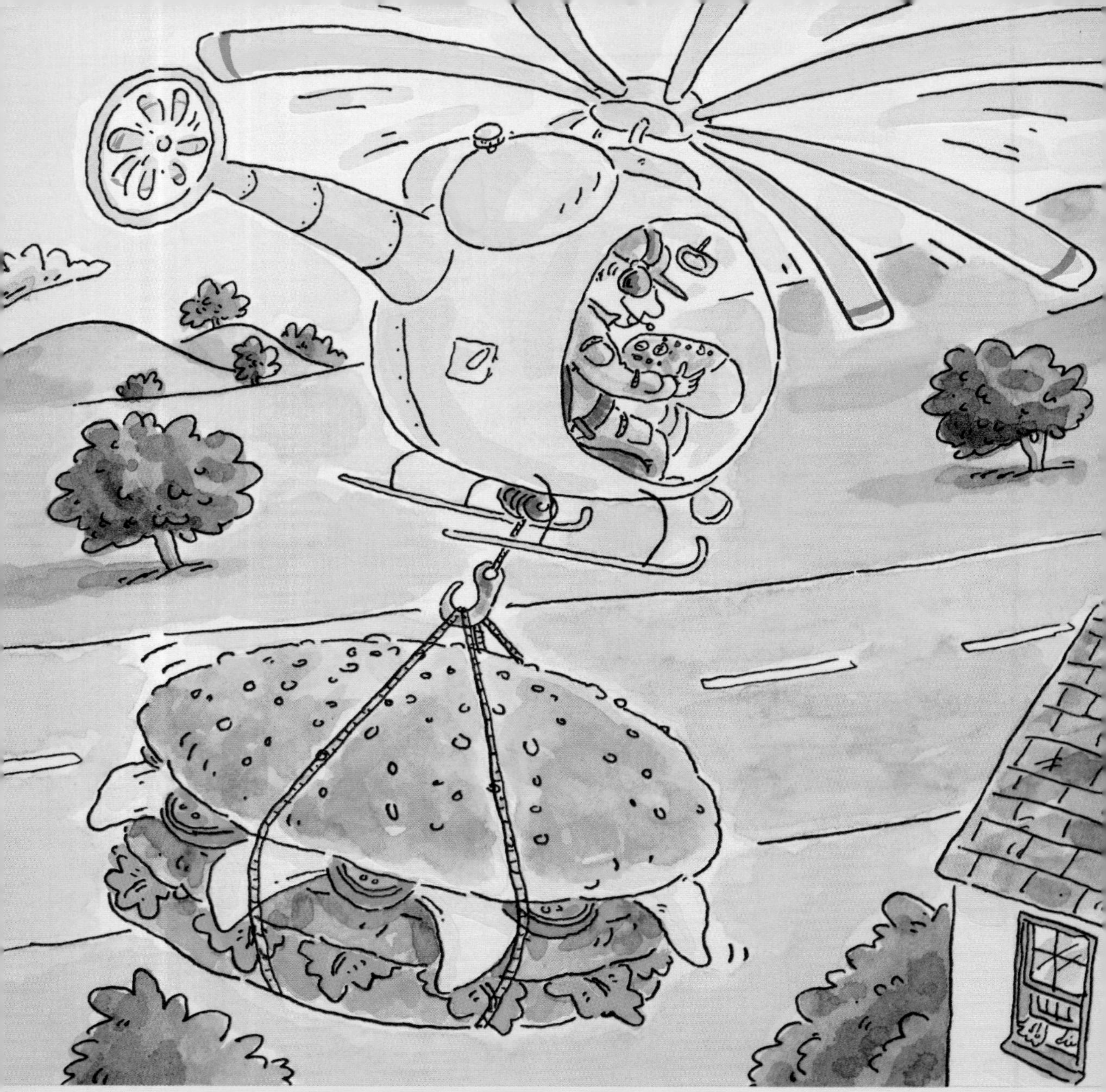

Huge hamburger.

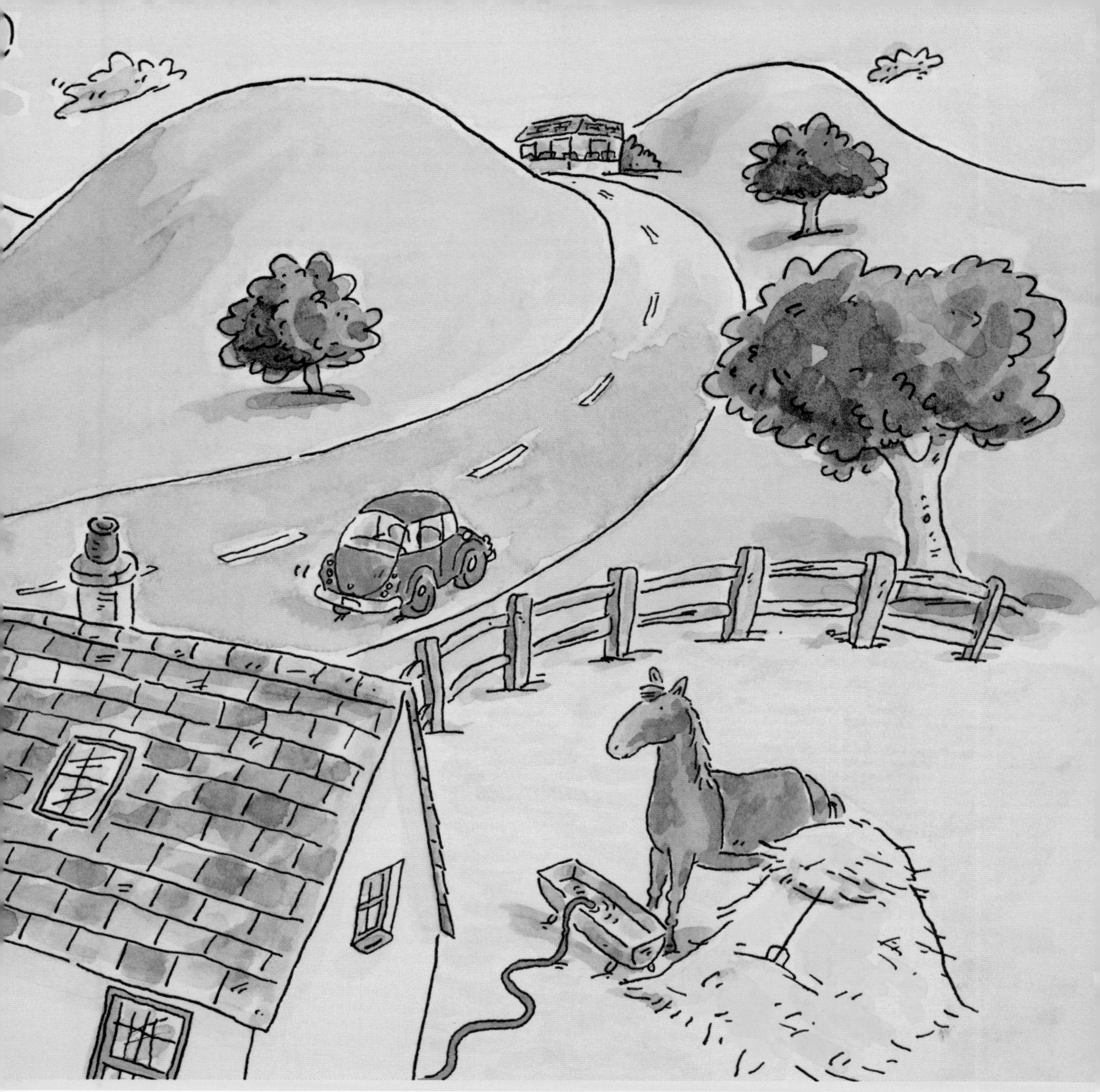

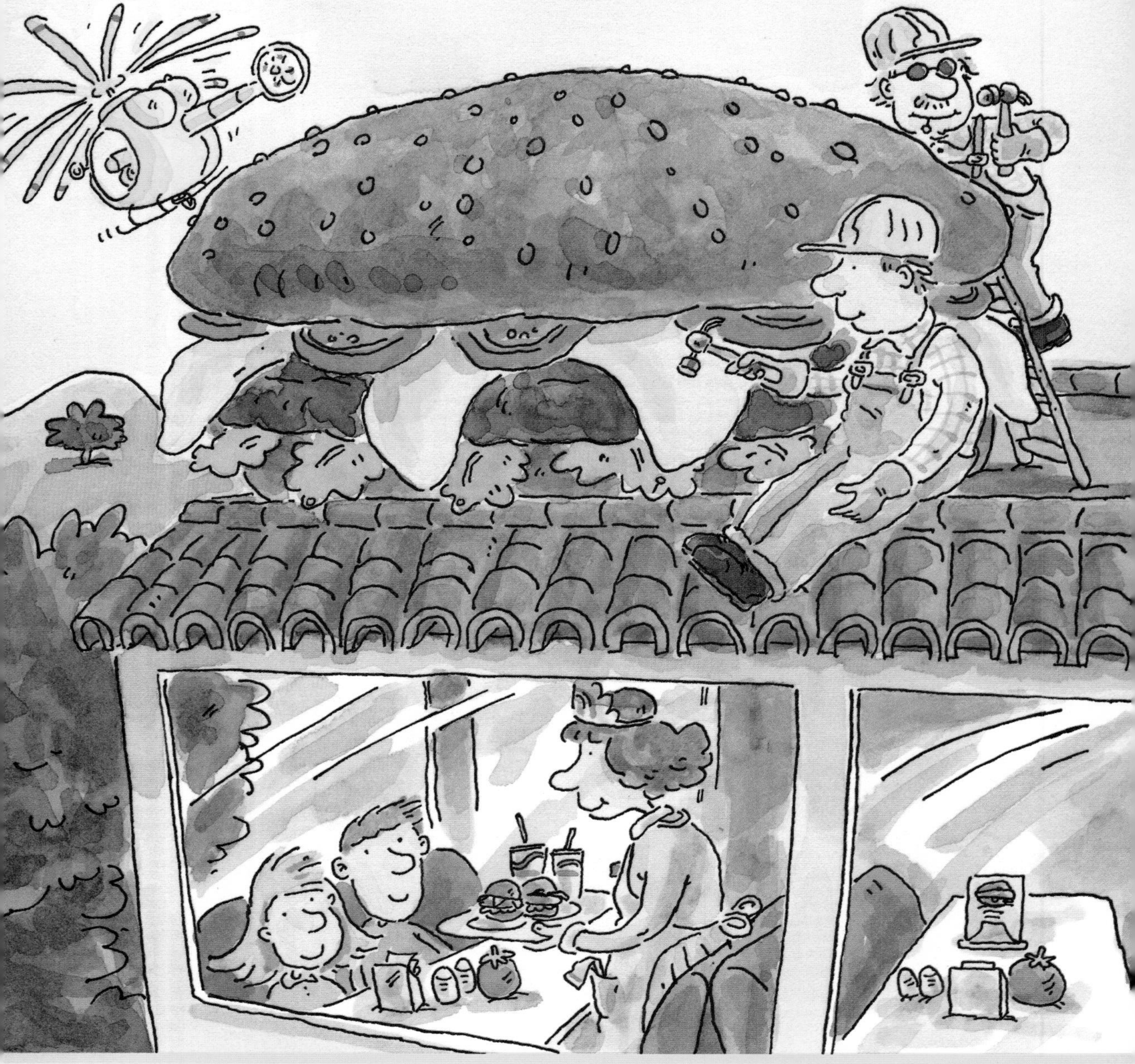

Huge hamburger.